A Simple Plan to Pay Off Debt and Improve Your Credit Score

By

Leslie Armer

Learn about and understand your credit report as well as how to get and maintain a higher credit score. Get out of debt the right way, quickly and easily, by following this simple plan.

Table of Contents

Introduction

If you have debt or credit card obligations that you are struggling to pay each month, you are not alone. You might feel like you are simply existing and not truly living your life. Do not fret. There are hundreds, if not thousands, of people in that boat with you and there are ways to get out of this situation.

Often, debt makes a person feel overwhelmed; feeling as if they are unable to do anything about it. Feeling stuck, they simply make the minimum payments just to get by each month.

If you allow it, your debts can really get out of control and bring you down. Not only financially, but emotionally as well. Having a lot of financial obligations can cause stress, which can lead to some serious health issues.

There is good news though, you do not have to stay in that situation. You have the power to gain your freedom by using this eBook. Put the steps into practice, gain control, and get your life back.

Please do not feel as if you cannot do this. Everyone can do this! You deserve to be financially free, so go ahead, take the reins, and get control over your circumstances.

If you remain diligent, in a few simple steps, you can become financially free of all your debt. You can live free from stress and worry. Live without those harassing phone calls from creditors pestering you for money. YOU CAN DO THIS! So, without further ado, let us get started.

Credit Report and Its Contents

Your credit report is a record that tells all about your credit activity. Potential creditors or lenders can pull it to make a sound decision on whether to extend credit to you or not.

They, however, should not be the only ones seeing it. You are entitled to see your own credit report. So, do not forget to pull a copy each year and check it out. You may find things that are inaccurate and can be removed, which will improve your credit score.

Credit reports contain the following things:

> ➢ Personal information like your name, date of birth, social security number, addresses, and phone numbers
> ➢ Credit accounts – includes credit limits, account balances, payment histories, dates the accounts were opened and closed, and the name of the creditor
> ➢ Public records – Liens, foreclosures, judgments, bankruptcies
> ➢ Inquiries – hard or soft inquiries made by creditors, banks, or other entities

Credit Score

There are several factors that significantly affect your credit score. They are:

- ➢ Payment history
- ➢ Credit Utilization
- ➢ Credit Age
- ➢ Mix of Account Types
- ➢ Credit Inquiries

Payment History

Your payment history on your accounts are the most important to your credit score. This tells potential creditors whether you are a good credit risk or not.

Credit Utilization

Your credit utilization ratio is especially important to respective creditors. This tells them how responsible you are with the credit that has been given to you.

Credit Age

The credit age is also important because it tells the length of time the account has been open. The longer it has been open and active, the better.

Mix of Account Types

Additionally, a good mix of different credit types is a good thing to have on your credit report too. This should make up about 10% of your report. It should be a combination of the following:

- ❖ Credit cards
- ❖ Automobile loans
- ❖ Student loans
- ❖ Mortgages

Although a mix of account types prove that you are able to successfully manage different types of credit, you should not intentionally go out and apply for loans or credit that you do not need in order to improve your credit score.

It makes up such a small portion of your overall credit score, so it just would not make sense to do that. To do so would just be irresponsible.

Credit Inquiries

A credit inquiry is a request by a business or creditor for your credit report information. They contact a credit reporting agency, such as TransUnion, Equifax, or Experian for your information. There are hard and soft inquiries.

- ❖ Hard Inquiry – It will affect your credit score. It lowers it little by little each time one takes place. Hard inquiries are a major part of the borrowing process when it comes to getting a mortgage or a car loan. They usually stay on your credit report for about 2 years.

❖ Soft Inquiry – It does not affect your credit score at all. These occur when you request your own credit report or when a potential employer checks your credit report. They can also happen when a credit card company wants to offer you a preapproval for credit. It is considered a soft inquiry because it is not attached to any particular application for credit.

Types of Debt

First, it is important to understand that there are different kinds of debt and they can affect your credit score in various ways. Once you understand this, it will make it easier for you to have control over your finances.

There are 2 types of debt. Installment credit and revolving debt. Simply put, installment credit is a loan that you pay back in fixed payments and revolving debt is money that you borrow against a credit line. Let us investigate both types in greater detail.

Installment Credit

Installment credit is a type of debt that is on a fixed schedule that you repay over a period of time. The number of payments is also predetermined. With installment credit, you receive the lump sum payment up front and then make equal payments, including interest, over time. Because you receive the lump sum up front, you cannot add to the balance, you simply need to pay it down until it reaches zero.

Some examples of installment credit accounts are automobile loans, student loans, and mortgages. Since these types of debts can carry high interest rates with them, the faster you pay them off, the better.

Revolving Debt

Revolving debt is any type of account that has monies you can borrow against, repeatedly. It usually comes with a variable interest rate and there are no specific loan terms. You can borrow money as you require it up until you reach your credit limit.

Some examples of a revolving credit account are credit cards, a personal line of credit, and a home equity line of credit (HELOC). These types of accounts enable you to borrow against the credit line. As you pay each month, you free up your line of credit and you can borrow against it again.

Unlike installments loans, there are no end dates to a revolving credit account. You simply pay the minimum payment by the due date. More, if you are trying to pay it off.

This type of debt is usually unsecured, and therefore, harder to obtain because the lender assumes a lot of risk. For this reason, this type of debt usually carries more weight in the credit score calculation. Which is why you should not carry high balances on your revolving accounts. Lower balances are more beneficial to your credit score.

Credit Utilization

Once you have a zero balance on all your credit accounts, you can either close them or keep them open. It is recommended you keep at least some of them open to maintain a good credit utilization on your credit report.

Credit utilization is the amount of revolving credit you are using versus the amount you have at your disposal. As previously stated, this will show how responsible you are with the credit that has been extended to you.

To maintain a good credit utilization score, you should try to pay your credit cards off each month. If you are unable to pay them off, at least keep your balances low.

You should maintain an average credit utilization of about 10% or below to have the best possible credit score. For example, if you have a $1,000 credit limit on your credit card and your current balance is $100, your credit utilization is 10%. A low credit utilization demonstrates that you are only utilizing a fraction of the amount of credit that has been extended to you.

Good Debt vs. Bad Debt

Sometimes your own financial situation is what determines whether the debt is considered good or bad. **Things like investment money, reward programs, or a consolidation loan are bad for some, but not all.**

Investment money is borrowed at a low interest rate but then invested at a higher rate of return. This should only be done by experienced investors who can afford to take the risk should things turn unfavorable.

Reward programs have some great offers from the money that you have spent by using your credit card. Some of these offers include cash back, free airline miles or tickets, and free cruises among other things.

These reward programs can be great for some, but not for others. For example, if you are one who pays off your entire balance every month, it is definitely a good thing and will benefit you. However, if you do not, the amount of debt you will incur, counteracts the rewards.

Consolidation loans can be helpful for those who use the money that has been freed up to put towards debt instead of spending it on other things that may be frivolous.

Good Debt

Good debt is an advance of money that is likely to increase your net worth. For instance, if the debt you are taking on generates income of some sort, then it is considered good debt. Some examples include college education expenses, home ownership, and business ownership costs.

Bad Debt

Bad debt is when you borrow money to obtain any asset that will depreciate. In other words, if it is not something that will gain in value or produce income, then it is considered bad debt and you should probably not go into debt to purchase it. Examples of bad debt are the following:

➢ **New cars** – Cars cost a lot of money, especially new ones. Although, we all need to get from point A to point B, it is a big waste of money to purchase a new one. It loses a lot of its value before you even drive off the car lot and you still have all that interest to pay on the car loan. If you can, you should save up money and pay cash for a used one. However, it is alright if you cannot afford to do that.

Simply take out a loan to purchase the least expensive, yet reliable, transportation you can find and then pay it off as fast as you can.

> **Credit cards** – This is one of the most unpleasant kinds of bad debt. The interest rates are generally high, and the payment schedule is organized in such a way that it takes advantage of the user.

> **Consumables and other goods/services** – Things like vacations, gas, and groceries are often bought using money that you borrowed. These things

depreciate yet you are still paying loads of interest on them. These dollars in interest costs could have been better spent somewhere else.

Pay off Your Debt with a Plan

First, you should make a plan to pay off your debt. This plan should include what you are going to do about your situation and how you intend on getting there.

For instance, you should pick a strategy, one that will work best for your unique situation, and then decide on how much you can afford to pay each month towards your debt.

- If you only have 1 credit card, well then, your plan would be to simply pay as much as you can possibly afford each month until that card has a balance of $0. Also, do not use it **at all** until it does have a zero balance. You may even want to cancel it after you have it paid off. Although, that is for you to decide.

However, if you are like many others, you probably have more than one credit card. Multiple credit accounts are harder to manage and pay off, but it is definitely possible.

Part of planning is to decide in which order you will pay off your debt. Some of it depends upon your personality.

- If you can exercise restraint and are a persistent person, you should pay off the ones with the higher interest first.

- However, if you do not have much patience and you like to see things happen quickly, then you should probably pay off the one with the lowest balance first.
- Another way to pay off your credit card debt is to apply for a 0% APR credit card. In doing so, you can then transfer your other existing credit card balances to it. You still need to pay off this credit account, but you will have a grace period until the APR goes up. This will allow you to save a few bucks.

- Consolidation loans or personal loans are another option for paying off credit card debt. These types of loans will typically need to be paid within 3 to 7 years, but they can save you a lot in interest charges.
- Debt Settlement is another method in paying off credit card debt. However, this is only best if you are in a financial position to make a one-time settlement payment to your creditor.

One thing to remember is that you still need to **make at least the minimum payment** on all your credit cards regardless of the way you choose to pay them off.

Strategies in Detail

Now, let us go over in a bit more detail the different ways to pay off debt.

High Interest Rate

When paying off the credit card with the highest interest rate first, you are paying the one with the largest amount of interest in relation to the principal balance.

In the long run, this will save the greatest amount of money, and, for this reason, it is the most recommended by financial professionals.

However, in using this method, you will not see results nearly as quickly as the other methods. Therefore, you will need to exercise a great deal of patience and remain persistent throughout this time.

Lowest Balance First

If you have small debts and want quicker results, the best way to pay off your credit card debt is to begin by paying the one with the lowest balance first. In doing so, you will see a much faster outcome.

In paying the lowest balance first, your overall debt is reduced. Therefore, you will free up cash and you are able to put that extra cash into another one of your debts. This is just another advantage of using this method.

One more perk of using this approach is that it builds your confidence level. You can see the progress you have made, and it makes you feel good about yourself.

A disadvantage of this method is that you will end up paying more money in the long run because of the higher interest cards.

0% APR Credit Card

You may want to consider applying for a credit card that has a 0% APR.

Then, transfer the balances from your high interest rate credit cards to this new 0% APR credit card.

This strategy will work if you currently have a decent credit score. You may be able to qualify for a good balance transfer deal.

Only do this if you have a plan to pay it off within the allotted time. Most companies will offer a lower interest rate for the first few months of ownership. Such as 6 to 18 months. After this, the APR will go up. So, make certain you have it paid off within this time.

In taking this route, it will help you get your debt paid off a bit cheaper because you will not be paying as much interest.

Here is an example:

Say you have a credit card with an 18% APR. Your current balance is $5,000. If you transfer that balance over to your new credit card that has a 0% APR for 12 months, assuming you pay it off within that time period, you will save more than $500 in interest charges.

That is a lot of money you could put towards your other debts.

I must **warn** you to make sure you read all the fine print carefully prior to accepting a balance transfer. Sometimes, there are fees involved.

You must make the decision whether they are acceptable to you and your circumstances.

Consolidation or Personal Loans

A consolidation or personal loan may be the right option for you. If you know you are not going to be able to pay off your credit card debts within a year or two, then a personal loan may be the right choice. Although not everyone will qualify for one.

In utilizing a consolidation loan, you can get all your credit cards paid off at the same time and be able to make one, easy monthly payment.

Additionally, this type of loan may help your credit score soar. Not only are you paying all your debts off with it, but you are also taking on an installment loan. Installment loans are much better to have on your credit report than revolving credit.

Revolving credit can be drawn against as soon as there is some credit available. An installment loan, such as a consolidation or personal loan, cannot be. Once its paid off, it is closed and that is that. Therefore, an installment credit is much better to have and will more than likely increase your credit score significantly over a revolving one.

I must issue a warning to you. With a consolidation or a personal loan, you must be responsible when taking on this type of credit. You can end up making your situation worse if you get this and then a year or so later, get another credit card or some other type of debt. You definitely do not want to get yourself in deeper than you already are, so **it is my advice to not get yourself into any other type of debt until you get this loan paid off in full.**

Once you have gotten a personal loan, **make sure you do not miss a payment!** If you need motivation, it may be necessary to sign up for automatic payments to ensure it will be made in a timely fashion. You do not want to cause yourself any further problems. So, be responsible and make regular payments.

Debt Settlement

Debt Settlement is basically a negotiation between you and your creditors or a collection agency. It occurs when you both agree to a set amount, a partial payment, that will satisfy the debt.

Usually, the agreed amount is around 50% of the original balance. This is a significant savings. However, you may end up having to pay taxes on the forgiven amount.

If you opt to use this method, you can go through a debt settlement company or you can choose to do it yourself. It is very easy to contact your credit card company or collection agency and settle your debts on your own, but if you prefer having someone else do it, then by all means, contact a reputable debt settlement company.

A word of caution though, there are a lot of scammers out there, so be careful when choosing which debt settlement company to use. In fact, you should go to the Federal Trade Commission website at www.consumer.ftc.gov to learn how to locate a good debt settlement company.

After going to the Federal Trade Commission website, click on "Money and Credit", then "Dealing with Debt", and then "Coping with Debt". Here you can learn what to watch out for and get a lot of information that will help you in your search.

Bankruptcy

If you have attempted to go all other directions and you simply have run out of options, then you could consider bankruptcy. It may be the answer for you. It would give you a clean slate and a fresh start. Only use this option as a last resort because it can totally shatter your credit report.

With this option, you will need to search for credit counseling per the Department of Justice and get an attorney. It can be a long, drawn-out, expensive process until its all done.

Information regarding credit counseling can be found at www.consumer.ftc.gov.

Two types of bankruptcy:

- **Chapter 7** – Requires you to give up some of your property
- **Chapter 13** – allows you to keep all your property.

Your attorney will direct you and discuss each option with you further. Together you can decide which one is best.

What Type of Debt to Pay Off First?

Understanding the different kinds of debt should help you in making the decision which to pay first. Although, there are several things to think about when making this decision. For instance, how much debt you have, the reason you are now focused on paying your debt, and what kind of debt it is will also matter.

If you want to pay off your debt so that you can raise your credit score, then you would probably want to pay your revolving credit, including your credit cards, first. This will improve your credit utilization and raise your overall credit score.

Something to remember when deciding which type of debt to pay off first is to always pay on time. Not doing so can and will destroy your credit score.

Put Your Plan into Action

After you have decided which way to utilize to pay off your debt and in what order you will be paying them, then you can put your plan into action.

If you have opted to use either high interest or lowest balance first, you can begin with the next billing cycle. Whichever one you have chosen to pay off first, send them as much as you can. Then just pay the minimum payment to the others. Once you have the first one paid off, celebrate, and then move to the next one.

Keep in mind if you are someone who needs a bit of a push, maybe you should consider setting up automatic payments. Just make sure when scheduling the payments that you pay as much as you possibly can.

To Cancel or Keep, that is the Question

So, after you have all your credit cards paid off, it is now time to decide whether to keep them or cancel them. When making this decision, there are a few things you should know first.

A zero balance sounds like a good idea, but in all honesty, it really is not. Having a zero balance a month or two in a row will likely not ruin your credit, but when it is inactive for more than a few months, your credit card company will probably stop reporting to the credit bureaus. If they do, other potential lenders or creditors will have a hard time verifying if you are a responsible borrower or not. Without a payment history, your credit score could be negatively affected.

If you want to keep your credit cards after you have them paid off, you should use them at least every other month. Do not charge more than what you know you can pay off within the next billing cycle to avoid having to pay interest charges. This will improve your credit score and help you to maintain a higher score.

Saving Money: Some Helpful Tips

After you have found the option that works for your circumstances and you have paid off your debt, it is time to begin saving money.

It is a basic fact that money is a tool that everyone needs to survive. Therefore, it is a good thing to try to set some aside for an unexpected expense, a new vehicle, or that well-deserved vacation.

Sometimes, it is hard to get started, but here are a few things to help you begin.

- Write all your expenses down – this means everything you spend your money on.

- Begin using a budget – there are plenty of free printable budgets online. A budget helps you organize everything you spend your money on. It will tell you how your expenses measure against your income. Do not forget to add in expenses that are paid quarterly, biannually, or annually. It contains different categories and helps you avoid overspending.

- Find ways to cut your spending – Look through your expenses and identify the things you spend money on you really do not need. Nonessentials like dining out, entertainment, trips to the coffee shop, etcetera, are all things that could be reduced or eliminated altogether.

Cut down on cell phone expenses by getting a smart phone through Tracfone, Cellular One, or Cricket Wireless. They all have smart phones that offer unlimited plans and are just as good as the iPhone you have now.

Call your cable provider and ask how you can cut down on your bill. They probably have something they can offer or maybe you can limit the number of channels you currently have.

Cancel memberships or subscriptions you do not utilize. Also, do not have anything renew automatically. Be in control of all your expenses.

Do not dine out, if possible. It will save you a ton of money if you take your lunch to work and cook at home instead of eating out.

- Start a savings account and set a goal – Once your savings is set up, create some short- and long-term goals. Add to your savings account on a regular basis. You might want to arrange automatic deposits with your financial institution.

Important Things to Remember

They say the way to eat an elephant is to eat it one bite at a time. This same principle applies when attempting to pay off debt. When first beginning, it may seem impossible, but do not focus on the entire amount. Instead, think about it in smaller fragments or chunks.

For example, if you owe $5,000, you could make 10 payments of $500 each. Most importantly, remain patient and focused. Do not give up! This is key!

If you feel like you might want to give up, come back to this eBook for some inspiration. Remember: You can do this! You are a strong and focused individual that has the power to take control of any situation. So, get out there and take charge!

Another thing to remember is when you have multiple credit cards with high balances near or over the credit limits, it will have a negative impact on your credit score. Take this into consideration when making the choice as to which one to pay off first.

Lastly, you must be on time with your payments! It does not matter if you only make the minimum payment, but it must be on time or the creditor could report this to the credit bureau and your score will be affected in a negative way. You do not want this to happen!

Conclusion

Debt-free living is within your reach. It may not seem so at this time, but it is.

Debt, whether it be revolving, or installment is so overwhelming and can ruin a person's quality of life, not to mention their health. It can take years to pay it off if only the minimum balance is paid each month. Trying to stay afloat in all that debt is not fun at all. There are harassing phone calls as well as letters coming in every week, if not every day. It can be devastating!

At least one of the previously mentioned strategies will work if put into practice. Stop living beyond your means, free yourself from debt and get your life back, starting today!